Make a Wish

Poems

Sarah E. Azizi

Copyright © 2025 Sarah E. Azizi

All rights reserved. No part of this publication may be reproduced, distributed, or transmitted in any form or by any means, including photocopying, recording, or other electronic or mechanical methods, without the prior written permission of the publisher, except in the case of brief quotations embodied in critical reviews and certain other noncommercial uses permitted by copyright laws. For permission requests, write to the publisher at the address below.

ELJ Editions Ltd. is committed to publishing works of quality and integrity. In that spirit, we are proud to offer this collection to our readers. This is a work of poetry. All views expressed within are Sarah E. Azizi's.

ISBN: 978-1-942004-88-2

Library of Congress Control Number: 2025935838

Cover Design: Tiphan P. Hunter (aka Tippi)

ELJ Editions, Ltd.
P.O. Box 815
Washingtonville, NY 10992

www.elj-editions.com

Praise for *Make a Wish*

In *Make a Wish*, Sarah Azizi confronts her inner angels and demons with brutal, affecting honesty. This is a fierce, brave book that does not flinch as it confronts the joys and perils of motherhood, the grave illness of a child, and the speaker's own evolving sexuality. These are not poems for the fainthearted, and yet throughout Azizi is convincing in her belief in "...this wondrous life, mundane/ and precious, all at once."
 —Elizabeth Spires, author of *A Memory for the Future* and *Worldling*

In this enthralling, important debut, Sarah E. Azizi presents "poems that fight death to the edge / of the page." *Make a Wish* introduces us to a single mother taking pride in the teenaged daughter who survived leukemia as a toddler, a lover basking in a panoply of lusty sexual experiences, a queer elder nostalgic for the time lesbians had their own bars, a friend relishing the company of others in her home, and a middle-aged woman fascinated by the changes to her body. Featuring poems as tough as they are tender, this collection explores harrowing personal trauma and large-scale injustices, but never at the expense of celebrating the small and large joys of being alive and the blessing of having "an after." In poem after poem, gratitude asserts its powerful presence, alongside the "necessary belief / that something good— / something better— / could happen next." When the poet promises that she is "never going to shut the fuck up," I cheered—Azizi's is a voice I want to hear more of. *Make a Wish* leaves us wishing to reread it and craving what comes next. I love this book!
 —Marisa P. Clark, author of *Bird*

In *Make a Wish*, Sarah Azizi writes to "rip off the band-aid of taboo." She invites us to sift through our mysteries and memories alongside matchboxes, sugar & spice, the touch of silk on skin, out of sight knives, hope and motherhood embraced, and the mundane gardens we happily tend. Her lush poems also affirm what it means "to be in & of this world" of desire, hunger, and sexuality. She gives voice and release to the fragile, abused, neglected, and the witness, carefully reminding us that our bodies are precious and "not meant to be camouflaged."
 —Juan J. Morales, author of *The Handyman's Guide to End Times*

Sarah E. Azizi deftly explores "The uncharted territory / of our bodies" in this exhilarating debut. Simultaneously intimate and expansive, *Make a Wish* grapples with the joyous, terrifying complexity of being embodied, from a daughter's cancer, to sexuality, to a friend whose disappearance haunts the book. These poems are humane and sharp-edged, shaped by desire and loss. Azizi writes "poems that leave / lingering stains" and will have you craving more.
—Izzy Wasserstein, author of *These Fragile Graces, This Fugitive Heart*.

In the opening poem of *Make a Wish*, Sarah Azizi writes, "I love/ finishing something off," but when her young daughter is diagnosed with leukemia, she must reconsider a way of life that has gotten her this far. The poems, bold and unflinching, are at their best when their music aligns with the moment: "here it comes, the trigger's/ firing from the proverbial gun. I'm on guard,/ adrenaline so thick. I fear I'll outlive everyone." The poems also sing through repetition and wordplay, as when she writes, "I will take, I will/ take you. I will/ take care of you." Eventually, the speaker reconsiders her earlier position on endings, "Let me be everything children/ are until they're taught differently." When she finds her place in the world, a place to share with her daughter and a community of friends, it feels like a wish has been granted; her child survives. In "Summer Party," the mother welcomes a throng of friends, each bearing gifts, until there is such abundance, she must attend to it. "I'd say more," the poem ends, "but someone's/ calling my name, someone is at the door—"
—Blas Falconer, author of *Rara Avis*

Azizi's impressive debut collection combines careful observations of life's mundane details with vivid expressions of the range of emotions they evoke ... The arc of the collection as a whole is a woman's journey from seeking others' acceptance to celebrating her own complexity and reconciling conflicting desires for connection and autonomy. Azizi's language is both matter-of-fact and evocative as she combines mundane imagery—dirty dishes, drinking coffee, walking the dog, "the sounds of cutlery & cracking joints"—with expressions of deep feeling. Rejecting the idea of poetic perfection, the author declares that poems should be "messy & glorious"; her poetry portrays a woman's life full of disorder and delight, at once wondrous, ordinary, and precious.

Fierce, tender, and frank poems that express the complexity of a woman's emotional life.
—*Kirkus Reviews*

for Leila Madeleine Berg—isn't it great to be the muse?

Table of Contents

before

You'll Never Be Bored 3
We're Still Here 5
In Defense of Small Talk 8
Connect the Dots 9
The Kind 11
The Big Sea 12
We Don't Win for Losing 13
Blood Binds 17
We Live So Much Longer 19
Then. Now. 22
Kind Conditions 23
Motherhood 24
Match Box Girl 26
Sugar & Spice & Everything Nice 29
Custody 30
Be Quiet 32

before then

Call a Thing a Thing 37
You Go Here 39
Cannibals 41
When I Am Doing Well 42
What We Save 44
In Dream State, he visits 46
Silk 47

The Way of His Buddha 49
Camouflage 51
Guy on the Left 53
Captured 59
The Devil Inside 61
Jealousy 63
On the Job 64

after

Make a Wish 69
Solitude in the Modern Era 71
Lifted 73
Exit 74
Strangers 76
Traces 78
The Dust 79
The Whirl 81
Fair Warning 83
Turn It Up 85
A Little Glory on the Page, Please 87
Apprivoise-moi 89
Summer Party 90
Single Mom Finally in Repose 92
Eventually, everything 94

Acknowledgments 96
About the Author 99

before

You'll Never Be Bored

A person's harder to keep safe
than a set of china thru a cross
country move, or a secret.
I'm the one who ends things,
usually. Breaks them

        off. Last time I cried for a lost lover
        I cannot say. My past's littered w/ headless
        dolls, chipped teacups, spineless books—
        a crack here, frayed edge there, til pages
        spill out & scatter. Suffice to say
        I no longer mind the shattered
        crystal. I'm not complaining; I love

finishing something off. The glass bottle
of olive oil clinks as it hits the drooling soup
can in the bin. I happily toss half-drunk flat
sodas, ice cream cartons, stale crackers.
Everything's got an expiration date. I blame
timing, list resentments, lose hope. It's not you,
it's me, picking the same situation again & again,
filling emptiness w/ the fickle light of love
when I know better. I've lost so many people,
what's a few more? I lost a whole country once,
& w/ it tongue & family. I'm foreign everywhere
I go, traveling endlessly, waiting for the perfect
fresh start, the nouveau go around the arc
of love. Everything's replaceable in this day & age,
thanks to the scheme we term *insurance*. I pay a lot
for mine, because I refuse to stop smoking—

I love the ritual: pounding the pack against
my palm, unwrapping & crinkling cellophane,
pulling the foil up & out. The crisp scent
of a fresh pack! The friend who taught
me to smoke disappeared

> a few months later—her purse, holding her ID,
> three dollars, & a set of keys, was splayed
> open on a residential road. "Once you smoke,"
> she told me, "you'll never be bored."
> We were eighteen & edgy & cool & knew
> nothing yet of how a day can unfold
> into a thousand tiny cuts of despair
> or distress, or at worst: ennui.
> No part of her has ever surfaced:
> not tooth nor bone nor strand of hair.
> I imagine she's dead, but what I would
> not give to know—

A heavy box w/ softening corners
holds every love letter written to me
before the advent of email et al.
The past is vast, harder to hold onto.
It's beginnings I crave:

> blank journals, dawn over the mountains,
> Monday waving from its firm perch.
> Every empty space beckons to be
> transformed. Throw it all away, I say.
> Reset! Look: my refrigerator's shelves
> gleam, brightly lit & blinding. I'll mess
> them up again soon enough, but I relish
> hunger, how it simultaneously demands
> & refuses to be sated. It's *meaning* I covet,
> sinfully & thoroughly, & meaning's tied up
> w/ desire, knotted in the spaces between
> fullness, carrying the promise
> of a resolution, an answer, an end.

We're Still Here

If only I'd named you "Rose,"
Leukemia wouldn't have been
tempted to choose you.
Leila. Leukemia. Leila. Leukemia. Le—
Your dad's mother was *Rosemary*,
dead long before he met me.
My grandmother's second child
was *Nasrin*, Farsi for *Rose*—
she died at two months old.
If only I'd named you for the dead,
I thought, you wouldn't be at the edge
of death at two years old, blood
mostly cancer, body invaded.
I could poke fun now at my madness,
but were my dark pooling thoughts
any more senseless than a child
having 24 spinal taps before starting
kindergarten? Your bone marrow, too,
docs scraped into it two dozen times
before your first school picture day.

How would your brain impose
order on such mayhem? I'd wonder
this, rocking you in the hospital room,
careful not to tug on any wires.
You had such rich thoughts already.
Complete sentences spooled out
of your mouth. Every letter, number,
color, you knew. Then chemo sizzled
your brain. Brilliance remains in you—
but I can measure what was lost:
a thread you cannot grasp.

Confusion ruled your life, distractions
got you thru, & therapy can't stitch up
what's been pulled & frayed.
Damage remains. The unhealed psyche
sings its own refrain. I wanted
to blink us into another world.
I wanted to scoop you back into me,
birth us into another dimension.

§

Today, snow has fallen for five
hours straight, will continue
into the night, blanketing
our desert home. You are drawing.
I am writing, about you, always
about you, to you. We are safe.
You are nearly taller than me.
I pull on a sweater, ask if you'd like
a cup of tea. I know you will say yes.
I know you will not finish it. You love
the ritual of tea w/ mom, you try
to learn to enjoy the tea. The kettle
whistles, water steams. I squeeze in
extra honey. We curl under an Afghan.
Your tiny dog settles herself near
the front door, guarding us.
I will never be able to protect you
from the deepest hurts—the cruel
schoolmates, the lying lover,
the institutions constructed to make
us feel less than. How long do some
mothers believe they can prevent
their babies' suffering?
That delusion was ripped
from me so early. But still,
here we are: my arm's around you.

You are warm, chatty, & for now, mine.
You rest your head on my belly.
I will never know the innermost you,
what you call yourself in the quiet
of your hollowed bones, the stories
you spin to create the thread
of self. Our minds unraveled,
no matter how strongly woven
we now seem. Our bodies push on.

In Defense of Small Talk

I've got a soft spot for the smallest of small talk.
Pleasantries give shape to quick interactions,
allow us to interlace briefly—what a dance,
when done gracefully!—create a sense
of safety in their predictability. Call me old
fashioned, but a dab of *Awfully cold today*
or *What fine weather* does work, real work.
So many don't get to keep the thread of self

spooled til the end. Small talk offers what the lot
of us need most but rarely admit: to regard
& be regarded. What a gift it is when a loved
one slipping into fragments & dizzy spells & flickering
eyes opens their whole pink mouth to say: *What a pretty
shade of blue. Nice to see you. Will you come again?*

Please, do.

Connect the Dots

Everything alive is tied to everything
else alive. The rustling leaves. The dark
red buds. The hungry mouse. The crone
in her last hour. The infant whimpering
at dusk. The spider weaving home. Tethers
stretch, contract, & I fathom it is *disappearance*
that holds the upper hand. How dramatically
it alters the fabric of existence.

                I'm careful
to water my plants what they need, no more,
to watch the soil soak up each trickle. I like
to wake w/ the sun, but once awoken I push
off rising. The house behind me's got a big dog.
His people leave him out so long at night,
I cannot mind when his barking rouses me.
Is anyone truly loved? Every creature
or person I've claimed, I've hurt. Maimed
a part of their heart. I find myself unworthy
of grace or forgiveness, which propels me forward,
toward practicing kindness. Unable to change the past,
                I aim to write
a smoother, softer future. *This time I will dismember
myself before I cause damage.* That seeming
wisdom, tho, can't be right, as any harm
to me or you, anyone, ripples out, relentlessly
entangled as we are.

My daughter & I have allergies so severe
we can't consider inviting a cat into our house,
but the neighbor's prances in the window
across from her bedroom, flirts & teases.

What light must dance in the thread from feline
to teenage girl on an idle summer night, paws
& grins, flounces & long stares. From where I sit,
I can't see their interplay, & physics reminds me:
if I curl up in my child's room to watch, my presence
will indelibly change what's possible. I satisfy
my curiosity as I always have, w/ a dash of faith
& make-believe. Between the two panes, I envision
a dazzling ribbon of light, glittery explosions of joy—

           & perhaps the dog barks
so long wishing to join in, but bound to the hard ground,
he knows best the song of longing, & he wonders
what happens when the windows go dark,
which to him means girl & cat & sequined light
have disappeared. Once again he's pushing
thru the night alone, waiting for some spark.
He'd take even the startled cry of a baby,
desperate for milk or touch or both. And who
among us hasn't been right there, anchored
& lonely, cold & so convinced the night
will never end, we'd welcome any interruption
to disrupt the solitary string quivering within.

The Kind

Let me
be the kind
who holds
the wounded,
picks up the tiny
creature, cares
so much.
Let the hearth
within me receive,
expand, receive.
*I am not my sister's
keeper*, my dearest
friend & I have long
said, no matter the cruelties
that attempt to swallow
us up, *I am my sister.*
Let me live
in the belly of truth
that I know to be
unshakeable: nothing
is for certain; everything
is sacred. Let me pat
& feed & cradle & tend.
Let me be the voice
whispering *hush*—

The Big Sea

Down the hazy sky the sun
slid. My baby's squeals punctured
the space between sand

& water. Dark blonde curls flew,
chubby hands splashed frothy
waves as she frolicked, decked out

in spotted ladybug wetsuit. Eight months
later her face would be rounder
than a dodge ball, w/ red flaking lips

& one eye crossed. She'd be bald
before Halloween. I cannot fathom hope
surfaces for a creature that cannot articulate

its pain. My dearest friend tells me, after
a childhood of assault, any physical
discomfort her addled brain interprets

as a new constant, body suspended
like a fish hooked & dangling. Acted upon.
I cannot recount how many needles stung

my daughter's flesh. Her eyes would roll
back in despair. Let me stay w/ her there—
toes wiggling in sand, neck arched to take

in expanse of birds in flight, mouth releasing
piercing cries of joy, & she wholly unaware
of what it means to be brave.

We Don't Win for Losing

Every piece of bedding's got a blood
stain, or many. This cycle of thickening/
shedding, swelling/ pouring, over 30 years

now & still I struggle to pinpoint when each
round of menstruation will begin. Last month,
a colleague lost her womb, which is not to say

she misplaced it, but that it could no longer
reside inside without killing her. That space
had held both her sons. She wants to believe

she's got a decade or more ahead, but when
cancer puts down roots, it plans to stay. Anyway.
A distant friend lost one breast last year,

& a dear friend, both. Why is the solution
so often amputation? Breast cancer activists
came into being because theretofore most

women afflicted would lose not only their breasts
but also parts of their arms, necks, shoulders,
& trunks. Which is to say, the medicine

of men could dream up no other way to defeat
cellular invasion than to deform the hostess.
Sometimes my middle-aged body sheds lining

every two weeks, all that preparation, pomp
& circumstance, the soft bed within me beckoning,
Surely, we want to do it again? When I went into labor,

among my most looming fears was she'd be slow
to cry. Not every newborn howls immediately,
& tho a quiet creature is not necessarily cause

for alarm, I fretted, would rub my belly
& beseech her unborn form: *Don't make me wait.*
That final contraction/ push, I quieted the hum

within me, listened for her voice. The afterbirth
followed, & on the heels of such encompassing pain,
I didn't feel the physical slice thru the umbilical cord.

For the rest of my life, I would, I soon learned,
sense its slow crackling, the reverberation
of every stretch & fissure. The nurse held her high,

my baby's puffy lower lip trembled,
& I exhaled as her fresh mouth released
a scream that delighted the midwife: *A fighter!*

A tough one, she proclaimed. I wonder now
how many wombs that woman had to declare
no longer, or never, hospitable. What does not

kill you may still kill your baby. When for centuries
those lacking a womb have codified your body
into mammaries, cervix, eggs, hysteria, I suppose

it seems fitting to remove, slice & dice, as if you
were the one visiting your flesh & blood anyway. Torn
asunder from the guest my body'd spent 41 weeks

creating, I reached for my red-faced newborn.
Her lips closed against my neck. Hours later
I cradled my deflated middle & ached for her return.

The fever I'd spiked during labor landed her
in intensive care, elevator shafts & hallways away.
The Western world does not hesitate to separate

infant from mother. I traveled across the hospital
to feed her, how I hungered to hold her—
she was swaddled in a plastic box, under staggeringly

bright lights, & a needle poked from vein in her skull
to machine. Delirious from labor, I assured myself
no such moment could happen twice. Whatever power,

if any, harnesses fate makes fools of all of us,
for not long after, the hospital became our second home:
her bone marrow was ravaged by leukemia.

The same chemicals that quelled her cancer
threatened to steal any plans for pregnancy,
but when the stakes include death at two years old,

fertility's an acceptable casualty. How desperately I want
my daughter's body to have options, choices,
as many as can stretch from one imagination

to the next, for it is far too common to be a woman
& lose your womb or breasts, voice or "virginity,"
femininity or fertility, space or sanctity. How much

division & removal can the body endure, let alone
the psyche? Not every wound can be stitched up
or hidden, healed or erased. The debased body

makes its case. So much of my life, I wanted
to disappear, secrete my body's functions
& render unseen this flesh I was taught to consider

revolting, never mind its dastardly needs.
Womanhood's a mystery, they crow, a forest fetid
& dank, full of danger; unmapped & foreign.

My aging body bleeds & sweats, demands
attention, makes itself known. I'm ready for lust,
to taste the heady rush of fear & desire, to descend

madly in love w/ my own form. My daughter's burgeoning
body mirrors the shape of mine. Every pair of panties bears
bloodstains. Her eggs, tests promise, made it thru intact,

healthy & at the ready. May she be allowed to do
w/ them whatever she pleases. For far too long,
my flesh & I have hedged our bets. Watch us put
it all on red, spread our legs, & take up space.

Blood Binds

The first time my lover cut me, my lips parted & all of me swelled up,
tender & full, as I breathed into the pain. *Your blood is so sweet,*

she told me as her mouth caressed my wound. How trite
& tawdry this feels: fantasies grow out of trauma. *Trauma—*

I admit I've come to loathe the word, it's become anemic,
which I thought was the issue when my child's body erupted

in tiny bruises, for her blood had first laced w/ my deficient
cells, but hers contained their own secret, silent malady.

After my daughter's final round of chemo, my fantasies ramped up:
I envisioned the thin skin between my breasts cut, a single

slice, blood dripping onto a pristine white pillow as an anonymous
hand or cock pushed me to orgasm. I'd trace the protrusion of bone,

scratch hard w/ my nails, slide thoughts of syringes & babies howling
in terror out of my mind. I ask my lover to cut me when I need to suffer.

Not every slice is sensual or erotic. Longer curved cuts screech w/ pain,
almost unbearably so. How powerful I feel when I push thru it.

My baby had no choice, let alone a drop of comprehension.
When my breasts are decorated in rivulets of red, when my bone-thin

skin weeps & blood pools into my navel, out flows all I render
unnamed, unclaimed. I revel at my blood made visible; for a moment,

nothing can dam its flow. I love most quick pricks, scorching & insistent,
the kind from which blood bubbles up, viscous & thick, binding. Blood cells

can't live long in the air—fragile little fuckers. I make them dance along my flesh, against this flailing, aging body—everything's got a limitation,

it seems, save for the meat of memory.

We Live So Much Longer

Believe that all the people in your life are blessed
    —Melissa Ferrick, "You've Known It All Along"

Mere hours before the turn of the century,
I won at Quarters. Me! The High Femme! My mouth
gaped in shock; the shot of beer spilled all over
my sparkling NYE dress, ruining the angora
(it'd made a brief comeback). But how could I care?
I'd impressed my andro slash butch friends, clustered
w/ them in my shotgun kitchen, mouth already buzzing
toward drunk. In those days, in heels I walked the three blocks
to the lesbian bar. I'd usually amble back barefoot, careless.
We had our own bars back then! The sub-zero nights
we'd wait outside a hole in the wall to snag
the best seats, see one of our own w/ her guitar
& lyrics that made us feel alive. Counted. Real.

    The spaces we could claim: tiny & falling apart,
but ours. There's something to be said for not having
to share. The nights we closed it down to AC/DC, my ass
shaking til the lights came up. The nights lost
to that constant desire to self-destruct. The glow
of the sunrise as we'd crest off the Expressway,
tunneling in from DC, where the dyke bars had more
than one room, how we'd be still a little high or drunk,
but ready to trudge into bed. I remember too the thick
spring air tinged w/ budding sidewalk trees & Old Bay
& fish markets, how the city & Harbor would fill up
w/ men from the county in their Orioles hats
& MR Ducks shirts, who'd never seen *girls like us* before—
them all salacious eyes & wet lips. We didn't understand
feminism well enough yet to be offended, but our necks
lit up red w/ pricked attention. This was before

they could order endless pretend versions of us up,
streaming. Real us I recall gritty, in jeans & tank tops,
spiked hair & dark lipstick, a little stained, always tainted,
mouth raw from the smoke & drugs & vodka & pleasure
of the night before.

    I won't live til the next century turn,
& as queers go, past 40 equals *old*. The faces
of the women I used to get reckless w/ beckon
in my mind; how I'd love to see them now & trace
the lines that must mark the decades since we roamed
in a pack, but oceans & state lines separate us. We failed
at killing ourselves, most of us, tho truly
most of us still try. Old habits don't die, they crawl
along the baseboards til we scoop them back up.
No one turns the first cigarette upside down anymore,
but smoking's still cool. I think of the women
who married men in the end, how far away
they seem in that untouchable country. I recall
myself in that fragile state, desolate & failing
at speaking that foreign tongue. How fortunate
I was to get out & re-orient course. I think of the exes
I hurt beyond the power of apologies. I see the women
whose names no longer come to my lips, tap
my glossy fingernail against my teeth. It's all
right now so close. Feels like I could touch us
in that club, put my hand on a shoulder & get
a familiar smile in the mist of swirling cigarette
smoke, clinking ice, spilled sticky beer; cuffed jeans
& black tights & voluminous shirts, me in those heels—

    I never did give them up, or the smokes,
but I've learned, finally, how to go it alone. Rather,
I hope I have. I wouldn't do it all over again,
wouldn't trade the daily metronome of peace
for the ring of the barkeep's bell, but tonight
the wind whips the curtains, the kettle calls,

& as I pour another cup of ginger tea, I conjure
the smell of us, clinging to each other in my kitchen,
then slipping into coats & walking a few blocks
to ring in the Millennium under cheap lights
& a half-assed spin of Whitney Houston,
she always fierce & full-throated. We feel endless,
open, the world of possibilities wide as an opera
hall's stairs. We don't yet know how rickety the future
can become as it spirals. We don't know that within a few years,
we'll never be face to face again. Someone lights
my cigarette, & the high flame of the Bic illuminates
our faces as we twirl & flirt, fling ourselves onto the dance
floor like it's home. My favorite song comes on,
we laugh, open our arms, & sing along: *How did you get here ...*

Then. Now.

Digging thru old photos
shows me I was a little
girl like any other, really.
How funny the teachers found
this loud-mouthed dark-haired
child w/ the weird name. I craved
approval, the smiling nods so freely
given to mediocrity, & at best doled
out in teaspoons to the likes of me.
I wonder now how a world
that welcomed me would look—
one without such class-
room violence. If I'm foreign,
what are they? Limited.

See me now: I'm scraping
assimilated normalization
from my mind, scrubbing
those chalkboards squeaky clean.
I architect my universe, invite
in the precious beings I aim
to protect. I'm tapping
my acrylics. I'm out of patience
for the bland teeth of American
veneer. It's girls like me for whom
I lift my arm to wave, to welcome:
Beautiful ones, come closer.
                Don't be a stranger.

Kind Conditions

for Stephanie

Over & over this image in my dreams: an axe slices
thru the air   I'm belly down
my lips the color of cherries   dazzling snowflakes
decorate my eyelashes   the axe

falls   onto powdery glistening snow
hitches its metal arc in frozen dirt   I'm warm
in fur-trimmed puffy coat   I'm safe
sticking out my tongue   to catch
    the kind of snow

that comes down only   in certain parts of the world
   under the just right   conditions

    & today I woke & wondered:
    who would we be if we had the just right conditions?

Hold her up   *the baby loves*
to see the sky   *the clouds*

Moon drop grapes   *are her favorite*

Keep the door cracked   *he's still a wee*
bit afraid   *of the dark*
      aren't we all

Motherhood

You clutched Santa so tightly he crumbled,
crimson glitter exploded, & your hairless brow
furrowed. Your lashes, full & sweeping,

were the only hair left on your tiny body.
Two more years of chemo loomed.
The remaining cookies I decorated—

not a single bottom burnt, but
perfection is too delicate for a child
who can't develop small motor skills.

Your blood was once mine, which is to say,
mine was yours. Somewhere, there's a parallel
universe where leukemia never crept into the marrow

of your bones. Somewhere, there's a garden full
of thorns & sleeping dogs. Somewhere, there's a button
I could have pressed to change places w/ you,

but I failed to find it. The dividing line between us
wavers, silver & thin, yet some give birth & never
feel this tie & tug, firm sliver of cord. My love

for you: a raw wound pulsing as I watch you dream,
face serene, hair fanned out atop your pillow.
I pace most nights, rub my fingers over questions

I don't dare pose aloud: do your bones throb
w/ phantom pains? Does your lost childhood itch,
entreat you to indulge it w/ a sharp scratch?

When you bother at a scab, how does your blood
taste, would you know if it came back? You recall
nothing. It was a windy day in desert spring

inside a fluorescent room. Nurses prepped needles
again for your veins. *It's procedure*, they said,
but we don't have any doubts: this is cancer.

Chopped clean, my storyline cleaved
where yours had barely begun. You ask now
for a clacking typewriter & stacks of journals

trimmed in gold. You fashion yourself a writer,
peddler of stories & human truths. I choose books
to dazzle your adolescent mind & pens that glide

like ice skates, make a holiday of wrapping,
curl ribbons against tautly-spread scissors.
At every crease & fold I wonder:

what tragedy awaits, what dim light
will flicker, then ignite into uncontrollable
flames? Every strange dream or tender ache

you express, I think: here it comes, the trigger's
firing from the proverbial gun. I'm on guard,
adrenaline so thick. I fear I'll outlive everyone.

Match Box Girl

Light from a match makes a candle feel more romantic.
>   Lost art: collecting ornamented boxes from high
>   end restaurants & hotels, plus cheap books
>   from gas stations. I had drawers full of them

for *special occasions* & *just in case*, but inevitably circa past
>   2am, someone (like me) would be so drunk
>   they'd light their cigarette on the gas
>   stove, burn off some hair. How tinged

that smell is in memory w/ joy & frivolity, youth & worries
>   that loomed like vultures, but from this middle
>   perch, I know they were shadow puppets at best.
>   The boxes I'd saved for prized moments that never

arrived—they all disappeared, got lost in one move or another,
>   which means I probably tossed them in a fit
>   of self-recrimination about how much *stuff* I *let*
>   accumulate, while neglecting to note that each tiny

carton held an intimate memory of its collection. I've got so much wreckage
>   behind me—lovers, spats, splits, violence (domestic),
>   divorce. Cops at the door, my tear-stained head
>   shaking w/ *I didn't call them*. Teetering toward

poverty w/ a little kid whose legs hurt from chemo, the two of us
>   in a three-story walk-up. Memory crunches like burnt hair,
>   useless, clinging, sticky. My mind's a junk drawer.
>   What can I salvage now? I sit in the solitude I worked

so hard to create & wonder if I've got one great love left in me.
    Is this, finally, what it means to be human—to fail
    so deeply you spend years in terror & therapy working
    thru *what he did to you* only to crave that same tight ring

around you again? *Connect, connect,* pushes some voice, but
    every dynamic, I end up feeling trapped in an airless
    attic, like I've got to protect my spirit from being snuffed.
    I don't do well w/ monogamy, I tell my therapist in a voice

so confident, I ignore that I'm putting the onus on me, once again,
    & not the tawdry system. Every love affair, I pound like a mime
    against imaginary walls, then wrench free to declare
    autonomy, & after this many times down the path, I know:

the problem is me. It would be wrong to knowingly entangle
    again, wouldn't I be engaging in trickery, creating
    the kind of enclosure I fear, while secretly
    palming a skeleton key? All I seem to do is lay

elaborate traps & prove I can escape. Still. How many days & years
    are we supposed to promise? Why isn't *I love you right
    now* cradled like a precious creature? I had a short-lived
    romance w/ a writer from the heartland, how different

she was from east coast me, but we were marooned in the desert
    of New Mexico, throwing ourselves upon the judgment
    of a motley grad department. I read recently her novel
    got published—the one she was working on 20 years ago.

It's full of her usual tropes, & w/ my particularized lens I can note
    which grew brilliant & which got tired, but I can
    redirect the same bright light & illuminate my flaws
    & gaps, too. Eventually everyone bores me;

my inner world's so rich. It's a brightly-wrapped gift, this realm inside;
    it's a burden, I suppose. And yet.
    A hungry flame endures, tickles
      at my tied-up heart & begs for one more

great love—*it'll be the last I ask for. Feed me the death I most crave.*
    Let the flicker of me be extinguished in their gaze.
    Bring me a lover who'll light my cigarette w/ a match.
    I'll inhale smoke laced w/ sulfur & sink into the magic—

Strike. *This time will be different.*

Sugar & Spice & Everything Nice

Let me be everything children
are until they're taught differently.
Tender. Soft-hearted. Easily moved.
Let me see always the weeping child
within, allow mine to step out
& reach for yours.
Let me hold your breath
in my cupped palms, whisper:
It is the light of you I waited for.

Custody

one

The first year's impossible: they come back
to you every week unfamiliar: slimmer jaw,
missing tooth, favorite t-shirt you've never seen,
once-beloved doll discarded. The light in their eyes
remains, but it shifts, & no longer can you track
them as a moving constellation. They become fixed
in time: your days,

    off days. That first year, you must
learn to feed yourself, & when to go to bed.
Each day threatens to swallow you w/ buzzing
silence & pain of waiting. You want to scoop
up every minute you're missing w/ them.
You toss, you turn, you crave the scent
of bathtime bubbles. Your empty arms hang

    & ache. Then, one night,

    you cook a delectable dinner,
flavors your children would summarily reject.
Your hips move to the music you can now
blare sans rolling eyes or sighs.
You artfully plate that meal & eat in front
of a show they'd never tolerate, one
you've wanted to watch for nearly a decade.
Three episodes you savor in silence save
for the sounds of cutlery & cracking joints.
You clean up, it's easy enough for one,
& you relish that you'll wake to a tidy kitchen.
Suddenly, finally, you feel tired. Bone weary.

You undress & manage to brush your teeth
before falling into a deep slumber, your
bedroom door flung wide open.

two

Silent mornings bring pleasure unfailingly,
like peach sorbet on a spring day,
or crisp wind & steaming coffee.

You thumb thru the calendar
in your mind; weekends taunt
w/ shifting meaning. You fill
your non-custodial weeks
w/ poems, friends, a little sex,
another show you've long
wanted to watch,
& there are times you resent
them being there. First year
divorced you could not
have fathomed this cloying
resentment, but here it is,
sitting primly
by the piled-up shoes
& backpacks, sneering
from the sauce-splattered
microwave. Go to your room.
Shut the door & breathe.
Count the days til you get
to be alone again. Alone
is all you ever wanted to be.
You should know. It's how
you landed here, week on/
week off, all tugged about,
in the first place.

Be Quiet

More & more I find myself talking about the blood
that cakes around my inner thighs now that a sizable
tampon doesn't last thru the night. I chatter on

about night sweats, my tender breasts. I don't care
who hears. My mother ordered me to wrap soiled
pads thoroughly, so my father wouldn't have

to see them. *What a waste of toilet paper*, I think
now w/ a snort, amid pandemic & empty
shelves. How quickly we're taught to treat the natural

order of our bodies w/ disdain, yet the distinctive smell
of iron in the blood never killed anyone. Approaching
The Change, I position myself in relation

to the world w/ this history of womanhood: I am
that which cannot be contained. I weep & storm
& flood. I am potential space. I alone plumb

my depths. I multiply. My body can feed
another human for years. I am soft folds,
radiant turns, fierce protection. My flesh

was a home, & I'd slice the heart out of anyone
who dared harm my child. These "scourges"
of womanhood—none of it's so bad once you

rip off the band-aid of taboo. I don't carry secrets
anymore. I'm unwrapped, spread open, excavating
the past, & I'm not ever going to shut the fuck up.

before then

Call a Thing a Thing

If I were a good girl, I'd leave their rape
trope undisturbed, parrot the mythologies:
Poe, the incestuous pederast we shouldn't

judge by contemporary standards; brilliantly
fragile Salinger, unable to fend off teenage
twig-like Maynard; Yeats, blissfully unaware

of how sensually he'd depicted the invasion.
How much could a girl like me reasonably
expect? Up until recently they could fuck

us at any time, sans consequence. Rape's such
a good metaphor: the swan, the golden God,
the battered body in the pond. I wanted

to be good; I had to pass the exams.
*To achieve expertise, you'll read
the works of these collected rapists & say*

*you liked it. Open wider, every page
gets a turn. Swallow. Repeat. All your hallways
& shelves are belong to us.* After class, I'd fly

back to my dorm in vigilant quick steps,
arms crossed over my breasts, lugging all
those heavy volumes, but I learned,

don't we all, to carry the weight
& maintain a good gait while I clutched keys,
sharp edges out. I wasn't raped on campus,

but at an apartment adjacent, & what was I doing
anyway, slamming shots of liquor & flirting
outrageously? Wasn't the male approval

of that cadre of liberal arts professors enough?
Spoiler alert: nothing will ever be enough, I never
feel filled up. I remember so little of those flimsy

Norton pages, & of the incident I recall only this:
waking naked next to his sleeping frame, cum
still wet in my cunt hair, my clothes on the floor,

covered in vomit. Nearly everyone, including
the friend w/ whom I'd come, had left the party.
I skulked thru dark rooms & in high-pitched

whispers woke a stranger who kindly found me
clean clothes, then drove me back to campus,
where we'd taken back the night. My whole life's

been punctuated by dreams in which my mouth
flutters open but cannot scream, let alone
form speech, & my body is laden, drowning

on dry land, seen & unheard,
unable to keep up or do anything right.

You Go Here

To be a little brown girl in America
is to be pegged onto a board, naked, splayed
& flayed. It's being too smart & not enough,
too thick & exotic, as in when the white
boys use exotic to mean *pretty plus slutty*,
to mean *this desire is dirty & all transgression
is your fault. You are the root of it. Slut.*

    The white girls know this & their hate
seethes out of their pink tubes of frosted lip
gloss. To be a brown girl in America
is to be the riddle itself, & expected to contain
the solution. Some of us solve the equation
by starving ourselves, others get big enough
to hide in plain sight. Both approaches equal
a disappearing act, a touch of magic on the lips,
sleight of fullness. How ripe for violence, the girl-child's
                                        belly.
Chosen starvation tastes delicious

& to be a brown girl in America is to be hungry
for someone who looks like you, smiles like you,
who is loved like you want to grow into being loved, who is

Lovable.

    is to be a threat to the social order.
Unknowable. A cypher. White Americans
want most to be average, to fit
                  in.
    How dearly they clutch their myth
of exceptionalism & demand the brown girls

pet its soft head. To be a brown girl in America
is to be an exception.

     is to hide, & if you can't hide, destroy
yourself from the inside out, in the aim
of arriving at *the median*.

     is to learn how to mimic
the traits of *unremarkable, simple,*
& make it look easy, from inside the display
                                box
of extraordinary fluttering beauties—

Cannibals

Knowing how sweet its meat would be, God
doubled the shell of the crab. In captivity,

the crab dreams of a third layer, unyielding.
Claws, oceans, & storms of sand haunt

the mouth of my dreams. Waves whisper,
What will the next season bring?

I dream myself in shells, blue & shimmering.
Salt glazes my thickened fingers as I slice

thru waves, toward you. Where is the line
between rescue & capture? If caught only

by claw, the crab can sacrifice one, even two,
for freedom, trust it will recreate itself. The crab

dreams of nets curling, one leg snagged, then cracked—
I dream of waves ebbing, my shells separating, muscles

growing thick as I push thru sand & silt. You call
for me. Leaving dreamscape, I tender my claws

for hands. Sticky w/ the cloying sweat of summer
sleep, I ask: how many ways can you touch?

When I Am Doing Well

my house smells like caramel,
smooth & rich on the stovetop,
cinnamon cider, baked apples,
& pork chops sizzling in a sauce
my brother crafted. Soft sofa
blankets are folded, weathered
leather couch awaits guests,
kitchen counters beam, & rustic
dining table beckons. When I am
doing well, I carouse thru pleasant
dreams, sleep past dawn, wake
to sunlight peeping thru the blinds.
I take my waking at an even pace, then walk

thru my home & spray rosewater in each room. I leave
all the doors open. I sip coffee on the balcony,
stretch then slide on sneakers to venture thru this neighborhood

I love. I feel so safe here. When I am doing well,
what's in front of me receives my unwavering
attention: my child crowing *mom*, a meditation
on the blank page, the tug of my future self.
When I am doing well, itchy sleepless nights
feel far away, night's drapery of stars & moon
opens the magic inside me, & I am able to let
my lover deeply in. When I am doing well, I forget
I lived inside shoulders shoved against flimsy locks.
I forget slamming doors & counters trashed
w/ bottles & caps, fingerprints & shame,
forget the stink of sour breath & liquid shit,
that I was ever hopeless & helpless, made
a speck under the gaze of a man once

deemed "husband." My lover glides
into my bedroom, sets up camp in my bed.
After sex I feed us chocolates,
wipe slick raspberry from their lips, kiss
them tenderly. I take the open doors
& quiet for granted. How daring it is
to share a favored butter crème, to tangle
legs while our bellies ripen w/ pleasure
& gauzy curtains swell w/ wind.
I dare. I do.

What We Save

I chose the ailing plant:
its brown leaves crumbled when touched;

its roots strangled thru the bottom
of the pot. I insisted my lover hold

her for six hours of empty highway. (Her hands
were magical.) To this day she thrives,

but of my lover I have only a box of letters
& trinkets. I tell myself only that which lasts

counts. But. What appears fleeting
is so often what remains. Lovers we expect to leave

stay; love we expect to keep
disintegrates. So little is stable. (Her body

above mine. Her cunt in my mouth.)
I'm beginning—barely beginning—to understand:

love, like the body, is only one kind of home.
We keep the past alive: a scribbled note,

bag of brittle petals, or trail of scent
can topple us. We stop ourselves

from remembering touch. (My legs open,
shaking. Her fingers

inside me.) Screeching after the ones who leave,
we are a demanding bunch—

how do we know who we are when
we become the one left behind?

Needing to save what can't be touched,
I crave just one memory unfettered

by bitterness. I am begging here (her back to me),
filled w/ desire for one

thing stable, one thing stable—
how we all long for one stable thing.

In Dream State, he visits

& from his mouth pink ribbons of Arabic stream,
snake into twisting vines as he calls

me *luscious*. His tongue, fresh petal, first kisses
the hollow of my neck; my legs sway. The air's thick

& fragrant like a flower girl's summer bouquet.
When our lips part, more ribbons—how they spring

forth, swirl into long-stemmed flowers, dance against
my blushing flesh, sink in, & leave faint

blue tattoos. Sweat trickles between my breasts,
& morning breaks. The gate clangs. He can't cross through.

Silk

in old English
seoloc
origin unknown,
tho likely Slavic,
ultimately Chinese

spun for centuries
by spiders
to create webs, nests,
homes

secreted by silkworms,
to cocoon, hide,
wrap

possessing strength, elasticity

a sign of opulence

& found at the ends
of ears of corn,
thin, soft hairs
we peel away
to suck upon
sweetness

the feel of your skin
my skin
the downy hairs
at the small
of your back,
the nape
of your neck,
rustling

between sheets
is that you? me?
which hand rests upon my hip?
which thigh rides between?
which soft tongue runs the course
of valleys, rivers, hills?

Silk
the corners of your thighs

Silk
of the nightgown
you raise
of the hands that unwrap
my cocoon

of the scarf that ties
my wrists so that I am
offered to the hands

that touch
climb into me
the silken mouth I ride
to which I come home.

Silk—
O, do not let
the tiny webs
fool you
their shiny homes
are not easily
broken

do not forget
that I am flesh, blood
but this cool night—
wrap me in silk

The Way of His Buddha

Desire is the problem, he said.
If I could walk the way of the Buddha,
let go of all this want …

I said, *What is it you want?*
He shook his head & I told him,
You want someone to listen. You want me to listen.

He said, *If you realize you are God
& God is in you then you can create your
reality. This is the way the world works.*

I felt sorry for him, sorry for the whole group of them,
meeting four times a week to meditate & talk about spirit.
All of them white & all of them middle-aged

& all of them straight & all of them at least
middle class if not higher.
And their guru, their great god,

in the same tax bracket if not higher.
He'd tantalized these people of money & access
who said to themselves, *What now?*

He'd told them, *Meditate & walk
the eightfold path of the Buddha*,
each of them blinded by the bright

lonely spaces inside them. But me?
I want to fall out of love so many times
I think I'll never write another poem,

& then I want to fall in love again,
w/ the wrong person again,
to spend all day baking the perfect pastry

for her birthday, to tell him all my secrets
over cabernet & cigarettes, only to have
the relationship collapse a week later,

for what matters in the end
is giving in to this god inside me.
The god inside me walks in high heels,

so she always takes the path of least
resistance. I told him, *Honey, the only real fold path
leads to my pussy*, & he knelt before me

& kissed me all the way inside until
desire was the only scent in the room.

Camouflage

He thought my skirt was too short,
& the rising curves of my breasts too tantalizing.
Can't you wear a turtleneck?

It was our third date.
No, I said, *besides, they don't
disappear.* Since I wanted to get laid—

yes, I am that kind of girl—
I grabbed a cardigan.
In the restaurant sat a girl as white

as him, her shirt tighter
& lower than mine, mosquito
breasts & side cleavage exposed,

pink nipples hard under linen. Everyone
smiled at her. At me, they stared.
I'm a busty girl. I grinned at him.

There are ways to camouflage, he said.
*I love your body, but not
the attention it draws.* Into dawn he dragged

his gleaming teeth & lips
over my flesh, sucked
my sand-brown nipples,

ran his hands up my thighs.
He pulled my lips apart.
His cock hung, dangled

dangerously. I convulsed,
opened wider & wider;
gushed, poured over it.

I woke w/ the sheet
around my waist, pulled it over
my breasts. They'd dangled

all night, precariously,
embarrassingly. His white body
lay naked beside me. I pushed

the sheet off me
& wrapped it around him.
Can't you cover yourself?

This is not a poem of self-degradation. Listen:
My body is not to be camouflaged.
This is a poem of telling:
My body is not obscene.

Guy on the Left

How pure we were then, before Rimbaud, before Blake. Grace. Love. Take care of us. Please.
  —CK Williams, "The Gas Station"

1.
We were the receptionists. Our name
was Michelle. *Hello & thank you
for calling. How can I help you?*

Our job: feign interest.
Six women, six rooms.
The sex was secondary.

We had our reasons.
Teresa had two boys
& a husband who loved

to hit her. Samantha had
extraordinary experience. Heidi
kept silent. Kelly wanted

to buy her kids the best
Christmas ever. Athena
owned us. I wanted

money, lots of money,
cash to carry, to never
again think, *Can I afford this?*

So much of it came easily—
I once bartered $100 to remove
my blouse. $150 for a brief

masturbation show. Athena
taught us: *If they want to touch
you, say you want to show*

*them how you like it. Pretend
you're in ecstasy, can't stop,
& fake an explosive one.*

We sat vigilant in the break room,
sprang at the doorbell's ring—first come,
first serve. The first to rise

opened the door, led him
to a room. Came back to say,
Guy on the left or

Guy on the right & we'd march
single file down the hall, open
the door, introduce ourselves,

extend our hands, the art of the deal,
show breast or hip-flesh,
wiggle on the way out.

2.
He wanted a blowjob.
She wanted a tip.

He pulled out his cock.
Shocked by how
shriveled & thin it was,

like half a Popsicle stick
or a crooked finger, she
put it in her mouth.

He exploded. She spit
into an empty candle
holder. He gave her

a pile of twenties. She
fingered the edges of the bills,
flicked her tongue against

the pad of her forefinger,
calculated the ratio:
2 minutes into $120

equals one dollar
per second. Later
that night, at home, she

read Nabokov, broke
the spine & fingered
the pages' edges, folded

a triangle to mark her place.
She slid the money
into the book jacket,

slept w/ visions
of tongues, the urgent taste
of cash on her fingers.

3.
We dreamt of cocks
& dollars, grimy fingernails
& sweat-soaked shirts,

our cunts swelling w/ bills,
coins pouring from our mouths.
We dreamt of banks, of our bankable

bodies, our breasts spilling over
the water's edge, into
riverbanks, lakes, oceans thick

w/ the taste of salt, of rubbing
froth down our bellies, thru
the unchecked territory of our thighs.

4.
Sometimes, tears came into their eyes
when we touched them: our fingers
pressing into their shoulders,

our nails trailing down their backs.
Sometimes, we knew how desperate
they were for touch. They would ask,

Is there a release? We would smile
& rest our hands on their hips.
How would you like to take care of that?

We'd explore their fragile bodies,
gently help them cum,
whisper thru our fingertips:

*I will take, I will
take you, I will
take care of you.*

5.
We frighten you
as well we should—

We know how to straddle
your white picket fence.

6.
What is the ratio of the dollar
to self-respect? The going rate
of choice? Does the DOW

drop five points for every
sucked cock? What is the supply
& demand of desire?

7.
Oh baby oh baby oh yes that's good, be a good boy,
you know what to do, let me have that sweet cum

don't hold back on me now baby baby darlin'
sweet thing, let me take care of you

8.
Spent, tongues grainy
w/ the remnants of cigarettes,
lipstick peeling from dry lips,

we file into the parking lot:
See you tomorrow ...
Call if you'll be late ...

Hours later, sequestered in our
bathrooms, we stare at our reflections:
we see objects of desire, from cunt

to toe, hip to head, we know
the economy of silence & smiles.

9.
I refuse

the prim experts w/ lips pursed
into fine lines, who claim
our choices are warning signs

that we are women *abused*,
women *neglected*,
women *working out our demons*.

We are the clutches of desire.
We are cunning & slick.
We mark our own borders, cry

Land ho! Ho! The unchartered territory
of our bodies defies infiltration,
exploration, the armies

of "sanctified" discovery.
Sailing into our own shores,
we drive in our stakes of claim

& colonize the harsh country
of our bodies' profit.

Captured

He has a new girl every week
but she remains his favorite.
He strews the photographs
across his bed,
rubs the glossy finish,
masturbates to a frenzy,
cumming to the image
of her cumming.
How she fucks the camera—

        I think of him now at such odd times—
        like when I catch my nakedness
        in the mirror—
        his tongue licking his lips,
        his pupils growing smaller,
        his thick hairy hands
        moving me, posing
        me, pushing
        the round black button/
        a green light
        a white flash
        a waving check.

how she bends at the waist,
holds her hips w/ her hands,
smiles w/ her legs wide;
& stretched on the floor,
arms thrown lazily to the side,
breasts taut, staring at the ceiling;
kneeling over sheets,

hair mussed, lips parted,
twisting her breasts;
on her knees,
supporting herself w/ one hand,
using the other to wet
the space between her thighs.

    I've come to think myself
    the corrosion of a fantasy.
    Tarnished
    to a putrid green.

When sleep comes,
all that remains
of what he does
w/ her is sticky
film, the white
gel of his orgasm.

    Only my image remains.
    I didn't stay
    in that house
    w/ those lights
    fucking myself
    for his beady eyes.
    Captured,
    I still win.

The Devil Inside

after D.H. Lawrence (and INXS)

I wish I were like the people
who would not pull
the lever, deliver the shock, take

the order & hope for the best. Yet,
I despise. I imagine
revenge, prefer mine cold, ready to burn

like a freezer full of white-capped ice. Grace
slips thru my shrinking
fingers. I'm small inside, bone-hard & base.

I'd get cross w/ the snake at my water trough.
I wouldn't aim to harm,
per se, but neither would I welcome him. Me,

who could buy water by the gallons, bottled
& spruced up. Me, who almost
always has enough to share. I'd not want him

to get comfortable. *It's MY water*, I'd declare, even tho
such creatures take so little.
It's not that I'd wish him death, it's that I'd want

him to be the guest of someone else.
See: the colonial inside me
needs to own it all & the colonial can't be excised

completely. Trust me, I've tried. Sliced & watched
it divide, multiply. I carry
such viciousness within. The cruelty inside me honors

the cruelty inside you. I've threatened, lied. Manipulated
lovers, made a fellow
little girl feel unworthy, cast aside. A flash of weakness

in another lights up the mean one inside.
Make her tongue flicker.
She preens, licks her lips, & grins. Her eyes

gleam. Admit it: you can't help but invite her in.

Jealousy

for Madi

an untended garden

thick vines choke
budding flowers

petals scatter

dogs trample tulips
leave roots in tatters

it's sticky, sickly sweet
the soil's sour

& all you have to do
is tend the garden but

all you have to do
is tend the garden

On the Job

My arm aches. Kelly's forehead glistens.
Not the rubber, he pleads, but Kelly
plies his swollen flesh, sweeps the tail gently

across the back of his thighs, then snaps
it without mercy. A flaming stripe bursts
across his ass. He howls. It is my first time.

I expect him to desire tenderness, teasing,
intimacy even. How am I to create intimacy
across four feet of leather? *Let it out,*

she says, *no one can hear you.* We've already
landed stroke after stroke. His screams ricochet
off the thin walls. She nods at me, prods

me to whip his body again. It is then, finally,
that I understand: he cries not for this body,
but for his wife, dead three years. He spoke

of her only an hour ago, sipping wine,
eyes cast down at Kelly's kitchen table:
How she suffered. He shook his head.

She shouldn't have had to suffer.
Hours of dialysis left her body wracked.
Decades of loneliness stretched

ahead. They had shared this for 30 years—
his naked body below her, leather
in her hands. *It wasn't her thing,*

he'd said, *but how she loved me.*
I'm agnostic, he went on, *how could I*
be anything else after what I saw my wife endure?

God may have left; God may be in this room.
Jesus, oh God, please, God, please.
All afternoon I've held back, refused

to inflict what Kelly did, thought
she was going too far, & I knew
better, but I failed at this job,

failed him. Flesh allows what the mind
cannot; the body grants the will to endure.
I crack the leather high above my head:

Let it out. I will be your witness.

after

Make a Wish

This lemon-soaked raspberry fits
the tip of my tongue like a little
hat. The heat of my mouth forces it
to melt, sweet & tangy. French roast
coffee slides down my throat. I turn
my face to the window, soak up
the warmth of the September sun.
It's so quiet. I'm scrolling.
The lit screen disturbs my tableau
of simple things, but I can't help myself.
I'm seeking advice, just a dollop. Tell me how
to cast off my well of begrudging sighs.
My plants thrive, the happy puppy circles
my feet. I stretch my toes. Such silence
before my child wakes, almost sensual
how it embraces me. With everyone,
I teeter between joyously, lovingly
welcoming, & put upon, annoyed. Resentful.
This quality I detest most in myself;
too, how unpredictable I remain, even to me,
nearly half a century in. *One day*, I remind
myself, *there will be no dog or child;
just you, maybe a plant or two ...*
My daughter's feet stomp above.
The counter of dishes admonishes,
piled high w/ the chore she abandoned,
per the usual, last night. I imagine
the counter clear, sink holding only
my cup & spoon, all of it pristine.
Will it be soothing, the simplicity
of a life that's all my own,
or will I spend it yearning for her fist

pounding until the flatware & glasses clatter,
her passion getting ahead of her, like me,
she the glistening apple of my tree?
Whatever's coming—peace & solace,
a fertile bed for my creativity, or longing
& emptiness, a hollow womb howling—
I'll find out soon enough. For now, more coffee
& a caress for the dog. My child's voice
disrupts the silence. I tune mine & call back,
arrange my countenance to show her, truly,
it is no pantomime, she is the most wondrous
being in the world. What I wish for her:
the sublime, secure pleasure of the single
cup & spoon. The tremendous feeling
of being untethered, & the certainty of being
sewn up within. What I imagine, rather,
it would feel like to know & trust, mind
to gut, in every cell, that you are whole,
that you yourself are a complete expression
of being. And if I get a second wish, it is
for her well to be so deep, she never stumbles
thru a shallow part, falls & flails, sputters
decades into nothingness. In real time,
her feet move from stairs to landing.
Morning, Madi. Hungry? The glass bowl
of red berries trembles in my hands.
Her fingers seek out one, & place
the tender fruit on the tip of her tongue.

Solitude in the Modern Era

Everyone's got something
smart or smarmy to say.
Much of it is too long-winded
or poorly paragraphed for my liking,
& I'm trying to practice quiet. I take
my waking slow, & slower still, light
incense & candles, play wordless music—
percussion & flutes, a single violin string
reverberating, Middle C held til it fades out.
I held my father's hand as he died. His hand,
soft as a pillow, couldn't grip my palm back.
His eyes & mouth stretched open;
some semblance of him scurried
& fluttered thru his protruding
rib cage, then relented, trapped
as it was inside his hollowing body.
The smell of death is at first
the smell of nothing. I was in the preface
of my life at fifteen, desperate to escape
the confines of youth, he the age I am today.
His body lingers in that bed, in my memory,
in the house my mother had to sell
a handful of years later. I inherited his keen
sense of smell, almost disturbingly sensitive.
Crayons made him nauseous, the scent
of impending snow, anxious. But how full
our home would be w/ the scent
of Persian stews simmering: lamb
& eggplant, chickpea & dill. I love a musky
floral, roasted vegetables full of garlic,
fresh linens spritzed w/ rosewater
& lavender. I buy rosewater

at the Middle Eastern grocery, pour
it into spray bottles I pick up at the dollar store,
tho of course these days I go out less & less,
& the mental list of keys, wallet, lip balm
includes *mask*, & probably
always will. The whole world changed
but so much seems the same—death's grand trick,
after all, is whisking the tablecloth off & putting
the setting back almost as it were. I miss so
many people. I go on. Sometimes I use up
hours without thinking of anyone I love
who's died. At night, I put the kettle on,
inhale & sip herbs & flowers, rinse my cup,
make sure the lights are shut off. Little
rituals protect my willingness to stay
in the world, cracked as it may be. I cover
myself w/ pink sheets, rustle my feet, sink
into slumber, all the while held by gravity
& the absurd but necessary belief
that something good—
something better—
could happen next.

Lifted

Let my life
in scrawled
missives—messy
& full—

lift you, remind you:
you are enough.

No matter how rough
or indifferent
the world appears,
love is always
the answer, kind words
rooted in truth
always the elixir.
Let life
be ripe
w/ desire,
dizzying, heady,
& lush.

Exit

The way a stranger notes your turn signal, slows
down & slides over early,

opening space for you to merge, that balletic
highway dance—

how when you first follow
a new friend you love every post: the majestic

view from her hike! the ducks at the pond! the foam
heart on her latte!—as if you've never

seen such delights before. We are so primed
for kindness. We want

to be soft. A child battered
by mother still aches for her approval, far

into adulthood, craves her forgiving caress, believes
she can best soothe

what she bruised. We come in ready for love:
we coo & whimper, beg

& fight for it, until someone or something breaks
that drive. Still, the passenger

in the heart wants what it wants: to take the wheel
at night—windows open, empty

highway, heedless acceleration.
To disappear into the hole of 3am, where yesterday's

long gone, dawn's pitched far ahead, & magic
teems. To find the exit

to the past, to rescue the littlest one within—
hot breath & sticky

fingers, tiny, racing heartbeat. Gently, brake.
Reach for her. Night air thickens around you,

around you. Hold yourself skin
to skin.

Strangers

Friends & lovers come easy, leave
even faster. The creak of a door,
the cigarette burning out, shreds
piled into a box, hidden beneath dust.

It's strangers I have a fondness for.
The questions come easy:
Where're you from? What do you do?
Do you want another? Now, where to?

Drinks come easy:
a White Russian, a chardonnay,
a screwdriver, a pinot grigio,
a Cape Cod, a merlot,
straight up, on the rocks, just let her go.

Cities come easy.
I drink to their names like lovers:
New York, Tampa, San Diego,
Houston, Baltimore, Chicago,
Atlanta, Phoenix, Toronto.

In each crumbling metro,
crowded bus, passing train,
I leave a stain.

Strangers come easiest:
bodies tangled, small forgotten items: cards, lighters, receipts.
I hold them close on the planes
that take me from mountains to coasts,
empty sky to clouds & rain.

Sometimes, in sunlight, I catch a glimpse
of myself in someone else. I want to be known:
to spread wings & fly over each town, each home;
to drop myself into memories, to have none of my own.

Traces

> ... she vanished without a change of clothes, without money, without a car ... Tracie Mosley's purse was found in the street near where she was last seen ... "You begin to wonder. It's very devastating because you don't know," her grandmother said. "You don't know anything."
> —*Carroll County Times*, May 1995

It is late November, almost winter; every leaf
has fallen; colors lie scattered along roads.
The sun is warm, the air cold, brisk—
perfect, you would sigh, for coffee & cigarettes.

Traces of you remained that first month—
the blink of the stereo's light; the alarm ringing daily,
breaking mornings w/ hope. Traces of you remain still—
the bar where you drank your last drink stands;

the road remains, where they found your purse, w/ your ID,
your three dollars, your keys. Traveling, tonight,
I imagine you as enchantress: hiding in mountains, crouching
behind signs, sweeping through dirty rest stops.

I see your white blouse billowing; your crooked tooth, the silver Mary
round your throat; your favorite song, the "Happy Phantom" ...
*if I die today ... if I die today ... I'll run naked through the streets
without my mask on* ... It echoes, from my car, everything echoes—

& always

I hear your quiet confession: "I'd never give up living, never
give up driving, my hair behind me, never give up the road,
the going." The going. The (never) leaving. The fading—as if
you evaporate more & more each day, become the breath around me.

The Dust

Let me be as delicate
w/ myself as a I would

a garden snake   spider
tiny bird   bunny

flower mid-bloom   or fainting
Let me remember

We are
Living
Breathing

Help me let go of self
& body as machine

in the system of cogs
& slots   Let me be

in tandem w/ the butterfly
& friendly beast   kitten

& cockatiel   the scattered
seeds   & summer weeds

Let me remember we are
all of us
marvelous & irreplaceable

as unique in all the world
as his rose   of all the roses

in all the gardens   & bouquets
sprouting buds   blooming bulbs

darkened petals strewn   crushed

we are in everything

even   & ultimately
the dust

The Whirl

It's so good to be in the world.

Sundry task lists angle for attention,
but I take my coffee outside, level

my eyes on the watermelon
mountains rising into view.

It's just past dawn.

The first sips slide down my thrumming
throat & warm me like the sun

on a puppy's back or lizard's tail,
like my child's hand laced w/ mine

once did. Sweet memories surface rarely:
her cheesy smile full of brand-new teeth,

the softness of her belly
under my dancing fingers;

wispy angel hairs tickling
my palm as I held her sleepy head,

carried her to bed; the curl of *mama*
in her startling new voice.

The best parts of the past, I've found,
must be bidden, which is not to say

they've been hidden, but that too easily
come the loud, distorted screens:

his face contorted, her cries each time
he forced me to leave. Shame can fill

the cup of the past. Still, what gets pushed
down during bare survival isn't wholly buried.

What a blessing it is to have an after,
to be planted here in a future

I once couldn't dare imagine:
feet on the floor of my porch,

child & dog silent in slumber.
The magic of words still whirls

inside me. How good it is to put
down the cooled cup & delve

into the day, to be in & of this world.

Fair Warning

Some days, I eat whatever
I want: bars of chocolate,
tomatoes soaked in spiced
aioli, prosciutto atop crusty
forbidden bread. I drink
coffee til dusk, stay up
all night, sleep naked, wake
well after the morning news.
I miss appointments. No more
plucked brows or waxed
thighs, I'm ready for new
skin. My hair's more tinsel
than chestnut; the lines
on my face are finally taking
root. I kept myself hostage
for so long. I'm done
being a pretty girl.

I wanted someone else
to release me, but the row
of hooks & eyes down my spine
would only open at my touch
& tug after all. I fingered
the buttons' edges, rubbed
their faces, honored
their ability to close or open,
secure or set free. They served
me well, they earned
their keep. I hold myself
so tenderly now. I breathe
deep & make wishes
on the moon. Wine glasses

sans lipstick stains clutter
the counters. There's dirt
on my feet. I couldn't
tell you when I last
washed the mirrors.

Turn It Up

My kid reads me the gate code: *9636-hashtag*.
I punch it in, resist the urge to tell her irrelevant bits
from back in my day, & wonder if I'll ever shift

from *pound* in my own lexicon, having just turned 44.
Last birthday for two years—I'm skipping 45, the age
at which my father died. I'm like a toddler pretending,

twirling into a disappearing act w/ my next
grand entrance all planned. Cute analogy, sure,
but it's not rhetorical, either, & is not the internal sense,

that steady metronome, the most trustworthy
logic of all? My daughter retrieves her friend,
they slide in & slam the car doors. I'm striving

to be unlike my own parents so I stifle
the reprimand of *not so hard*. My kid's eyes gleam
when I let her pick the music, those mono-fold

almonds shaped like my father's. Hers hazel, his dark
as espresso beans, & I wonder what he'd think
of the hashtags & names, or the way we live since

Sept of oh-one. Slowly, the exit gate deigns to open,
we turn onto the main road, & some narrative dalliances,
I know, are better left undeveloped. Some curiosities

can't be fed. The kids bounce as I sing along
to their nouveau pop songs, & tho so often I've got
something to say, I quiet my inner hum,

let this present moment thrum, & tell my passengers:
Turn it up. Little faces, how they beam. The highway
sprawls ahead. It's easy, today, to leave the rest unsaid.

A Little Glory on the Page, Please

Written in response to an ad for a workshop that promises the student will leave w/ "ten perfect poems"

I need poems that fish pants out
of the clean but never-folded pile, poems
so creased they can't be ironed smooth.
Read me poems that burst into tears
at the breakfast table, sob into their cereal,
dribble milk onto their wrinkled, untucked
shirts. Hand me crinkled pages, poems
that struggle w/ the alphabet, always put "O"
after "P," think "Q" shouldn't need "U" all
the goddamn time. Give me upside down
poems, stanzas hard-shelled & towering
like broken vending machines, poems
w/ unshakable attitude & charm so thick
they might nosedive into arrogance.
I like a poem I've got to keep an eye on,

one w/ lines that hit like liquid acid
or rails of white powder. Fuck placebo
poems. Tease me w/ poems that leave
lingering stains: spills of merlot, smears
of lipstick, haunting coffee cup circles,
each mark a whirl of memory. A flicked
cherry from a cigarette makes a poem
sharper. A touch of ash & smudge
of golden tea lend character.
Let those poems leave dirty clothes
on the floor, sleep in sex-soaked sheets,
use the same cup after just a rinse,
never a full wash. Screw perfect poems,
all lined up like automatons. We need

poems that fight death to the edge
of the page! Make those poems messy
& glorious. Let them gulp air, from title to last
line. Feed me a live one, a poem flailing & wet,

desperate, naked, obscene. Mean every word.
I'll read that poem so hard, I'll savor
every turn, & lick my fingers clean.

Apprivoise-moi

When at the precipice
of menopause
by surprise
I fell in love
I said
Be wild with me
and they said
Yes
I said
Tame me
They said Yes
I said
Let me tame you
They said I like
to bite
I said I love
to bleed

Summer Party

My lover's slicing peaches
at the counter, towel slung
over their shoulder. I crave
the prick of that knife on my throat,
relish the smell of my blood, proof
that I am still flesh, contained
and free, aware of how much
& how little time I've got left.
I'm obsessed w/ opposites,
their unchecked
power. Death could be
the end of opposites,
or the most extreme

of them all. I drizzle honey, sprinkle
cinnamon, plate the peaches, & invite
my lover to lick the sticky off my fingers.
The doorbell rings & rings because

I decided, recently,

to live. To live & live, to fill
these rooms w/ music & laughter,
cigar smoke & toppled glasses. I suck
my thumb clean & my blue dress twirls
around my thick thighs as I open the door.
J's got cigars in hand. F's carrying a case
of ginger beers. M remembered limes,
& the other M, our favorite gin.
N's little purse holds all the weed
we'll need, & then some. My house is
where the good things happen.

My lover squeezes my hips
as I cut flower stems & vase another
blooming bouquet. These rooms are tulips
& snake plants, scuff marks & crumbs.
I've waited so long to savor the sweet
glaze of risk, to embrace the frivolous,
to heed less & love the wanton in me more.

I'd say more, but someone's
calling my name, someone is at the door—

Single Mom Finally in Repose

A father & son are having
a water balloon fight.
They invite me to join,
but I've got the skittish dog
w/ me, the one who took
a good six years to trust us.
I shake my head, & we weave
our way up the path.
New parents push
their baby in a swing
& my inner mother hears
the cries as more scared
than excited, but I quiet
the impulse to intercede.
They slow down into a game
of peek-a-boo, & little one coos
as we come around the bend.

I'd be over the moon to push
my chunky baby in a swing
again, but I feel lucky
enough where we're at. I take
care of us, no man's around
to hover or critique,
& the seasons turn so fast.
Summer's cresting, but before
the light goes dim at dusk
hot air balloons will bloom
thru the New Mexico sky.
I open the gate to our yard
& crouch to unleash
our supreme listener. *Maybe,*

I tell her cocked head,
graying beard, & wild
brows, *this year I'll ride one.*
My kid peeks thru the blinds,
flings open the door, & rushes
to spill the teenage tea I missed
in the hour just past. I slide off
my sneakers & take it all in:
this brilliant stream of sound;
our tidy, private space;
these prime years of motherhood;
the joy of being in one place.

Eventually, everything

arrives at its end: a pointy edge,
a clean & soundless drop, a final
phrase in a series of tissue-thin pages.
I'm quickening toward mine,

but there's a lot of life still in the morning
chores: dishes dried & put back
in their slots, sink scrubbed to a shine,
floor swept so clean of dog hair & crumbs,

my bare feet glide. That, too—walking, at dawn
or dusk—holds such quiet promise. Still so full
of surprise the same terrain can be; I want always
to retain my sense of curiosity. Much living

resides in the third cup of coffee, steam rising
from the favored mug—mine's chipped,
shows potted cacti laughing above the scrawled words,
You can't sit with us, imitates a joke

I've long shared w/ friends I'll likely outlive,
their bodies young but already carrying such
untenable pain. So much rolls around
in a stolen hour spent silent on the porch,

followed by, perhaps, a jaunt to the discount
store to buy plastic tubs in a fresh color for spring
cleaning, trashy paperbacks that'll wind up
on the already overstuffed bookcase, & faux

flowers to lay across a windowsill. Those silk
petals will collect dust, but so will I. Look—suddenly

I need a dish towel imprinted w/ a round
mustached chef, a plastic ladle in brilliant green.

I want to bloom, tend gently & breathe
joyously, in my clean, well-lighted space,
until at last the humming vibrant grass opens up to swallow
you, me, us, & this wondrous life, mundane
                                 & precious, all at once.

Acknowledgments

Mil gracias to everyone who published my work, who believes my work needs to be read by more & more people. On that note, the following poems, in various iterations, appeared in these publications:

You'll Never Be Bored (as Denouement) & Fair Warning – *Emerge Literary Journal*, nominated for Best of the Net

Connect the Dots – *9 Mile Magazine*

The Big Sea & Cannibals – *The Tide Rises* (thetiderises.org) – Cannibals appears in *The Pearl*, their first print anthology

Match Box Girl; Then. Now. (as Elementary Graduation); Kind Conditions; & Turn It Up – *The Coop*

We're Still Here; Motherhood (as Crumbs); You Go Here; In Dream State, he visits; & Strangers – *Fahmidan* (fahmidan.net)

We Live So Much Longer Now – *the winnow magazine* (now defunct); poem nominated for Best of the Net

Be Quiet – *Held* (heldmagazine.com)

What We Save – *red*. (now defunct)

Call a Thing a Thing – *Free State Review*

Camouflage & The Way of His Buddha – *34th Parallel*

On the Job – *Wrongdoing Magazine*; poem nominated for a Pushcart

Solitude in the Modern Era – *Rituals* from Bell Press

Silk – *Clean Sheets* (now defunct)

We Don't Win for Losing & Blood Binds – *Ghosts not Spirits* from Querencia Press

Traces – *Blue Mesa Review*

Single Mom Finally in Repose – *Rattle*

I am blessed to be someone who not only loves people (their mysteries & rhythms, the gaps between how they know themselves & how they are known) but is also surrounded by those who love her. My deepest gratitude to my writing partner extraordinaire, who calls me her "first & best reader," who lets me run wild on her poems, who shows me where to close buttons on mine & simultaneously allow meaning to fly expansively like a baby bird finding out the sky has no roof: Dr Marisa P Clark. You should read her book(s), too.

To my daughter, Leila Madeleine Berg, who at age twelve guffawed that I'd written enough for a couple of books but done nothing w/ the pages; who, when I disparaged my talent, took my favorite pens for a day; & who inspires me endlessly to be a little less perfect & a little more wonderful. And to your sweet snaggle-toothed, brown-eyed dog, Isabella Azizi Berg, who appears in so many of these poems that she'll be immortalized beyond all of us, as it should be.

To my partner, the incredible prolific artist, about whom I marvel, *There is nothing they cannot bring to life on the canvas, draw or paint or render*, Tiphan P Hunter, who created the cover art, who lovingly wants to see my rawest drafts & rawest self. Our creative coffee shop afternoons, replete w/ two caffeinated drinks each, are just the tip of the relationship I did not dare dream of, or know to ask for, that we have & continue to build. I aim to master my craft like you have mastered yours.

To my beloved closest friends, both of over 20 years, who take the best of me as fact, turn the worst of me into delightful humor, show me the most intricate & fascinating prisms of themselves, & whose elation for any of my successes rivals mine: Dr Michelle P Baca & Liam Archer Westgate.

To my community of friends & supporters, in no order other than alphabetical: Bernard Balizet, Chelsea Berg, Lizzie Derrington, Blas Falconer, Jenn Ghivan, Stephanie Huffman, Fiadh Leigh, Steven Melero, Rudy Montoya,

Frida Moreno, Juan Morales, Peter Ramos, E.I. Saint, Nina Salters, Shelby Sue, & Izzy Wasserstein ...

To the teachers who taught me to read more closely, lineate thoughtfully, stretch into uncomfortable territory, & write about what I want to know: Elizabeth Spires, Madison Smartt Bell, Lisa D Chávez, & Daniel Mueller.

To the writers who made me want to do this thing in the first place: Amiri Baraka & June Jordan. Please read their work, especially now.

With gratitude to Melissa Ferrick for decades of music that pushed me to be more truthful in my writing, & for kindly allowing me to use a line of hers.

To the staff at ELJ-Editions, w/ special thanks to Keith Powell, & w/ heaping spoonfuls of gratitude to Ariana, who, upon listening to me ramble about wanting the truth if any of my poems should be removed from the final book said, calmly, *I would not have accepted the manuscript if I thought it was bad.* Note taken!

To everyone involved in the production of this book & in the production of me: my biological family that spans continents, my family of choice, my queer & Leather family networks in Albuquerque & beyond ...

Thank you. I did it *with you*. Thank you.

About the Author

Sarah E. Azizi was born in Shiraz, city of poets and roses, during the last hour of July in 1976. Two years later, she arrived in the United States. Sarah received her BA from Goucher College in the chic 90s; since 2002 she's lived in New Mexico, where she snagged an MFA and has rooted herself as a queer activist and educator. Her work has appeared in *Blue Mesa Review, Fahmidan Journal, The Tide Rises, Wrongdoing Magazine, Nine Mile, The Coop, Emerge Literary Journal, Free State Review, Rattle,* and other wonderful publications. Sarah has had poems anthologized in *Rituals* from Bell Press and *Not Ghosts but Spirits* from Querencia Press. *Make a Wish* is her debut collection. She lives with her daughter, among friends, family of choice, and piles of unfinished work. Follow her all over: @SEAziziWrites.

www.ingramcontent.com/pod-product-compliance
Lightning Source LLC
Chambersburg PA
CBHW031411160426
43196CB00007B/973